HOW TO START, MANAGE, AND PROSPER WITH A NONPROFIT

NOURA ALMASRI

ISBN: 979-8-9885182-4-2

Library of Congress: Pending

Atlanta, GA

DEDICATION

I dedicate this book to my late father, the pillar of strength and support in my life. His unwavering belief in me and his guidance have been the foundation upon which I have built my journey. Though he is no longer with us, his spirit lives on in every page of this book.

To my mother, the eternal cheerleader of my growth and dreams, I express my deepest gratitude. Her boundless love, encouragement, and sacrifices have shaped the person I am today. Her unwavering faith in me has given me the courage to chase my

aspirations fearlessly.

I dedicate this book to my two incredible kids, Diya and Lana, who have been my

Constant companions throughout this challenging yet rewarding journey. Your love, support, and understanding have been my inspiration to overcome obstacles and pursue my passion for making a positive impact in the world.

Finally, I dedicate this book to YOU, the reader. My intention is to provide you with valuable insights and knowledge that will empower you to make informed decisions before embarking on your nonprofit journey.

May this book serve as a guiding light and help you create the impact you are truly seeking.

ACKNOWLEDGEMENT

I would like to extend my heartfelt thanks to *Marilyn E. Porter*, my publisher, for her invaluable support and dedication in bringing this book to life. I am immensely grateful for her expertise and belief in my work.

I am deeply grateful to *Dr. Cozette White* for the opportunity to coauthor Tax Strategies for Small Businesses, your trust in me and willingness to share your knowledge have been instrumental in making my authorship dream a reality.

To my coach, *Crysta Tyus*, thank you for believing in me and showing me that building a virtual business is possible. Your guidance and unwavering support have been crucial to my success.

Additionally, I would like to express my gratitude to the nonprofit leaders with whom I have had the privilege of working, learning, and growing. Your passion and commitment to making a difference in the world have been a constant source of inspiration.

Lastly, I am deeply grateful to the resilient *Syrian people*, whose remarkable stories and unwavering spirit have ignited my passion for creating positive change. Your resilience and strength continue to motivate me to strive for a better world through the nonprofit sector.

TABLE OF CONTENTS

MY JOURNEY

I was a single mom working full time in corporate America and going to school part time to finish my master's degree. I was living an ordinary life with my two little kids.

It wasn't until the Arab Spring of 2011 that my focus started to change. As a Syrian immigrant, born and raised, I was profoundly affected by the revolution that took over my home region. Worried about the state of my homeland, I began speaking publicly against the violence and fundraising for nonprofits to support citizens on the ground.

The event in Syria was deeply close to my heart! I could not look away and pretend as if nothing was happening!

I moved to Chicago promptly after graduating from Damascus University with a Business Administration degree in November of 2000. I came with my ex-husband and the father of my kids who had already lived in Chicago. After I had my daughter, less than three years later, I decided to get a divorce. That was the start of my *journey* as a single mom raising Diya, who was 18 months old at that time, and Lana who was 6 months old. The *journey* was not easy, but it was definitely rewarding, especially when I see who I became because of it and how my kids grew to be smart young adults who go to college, are active in the community, and are starting their career path.

Like many others who have immigrated to the U.S,, I could not go home until years later. It was 2008 when I decided to go home and attend my brother's wedding. Traveling back to Syria after 8 long years as a single mom with two little kids, Diya and Lana, was not easy. My son, Diya, was 7 years old, and my daughter, Lana, was 5 at that time. For them, that was their first time on a plane for such a long trip. I was nervous, scared, and anxious. I was not sure how I was going to handle the layover in Amman, Jordan. When we arrived at Amman, Jordan, I had to drag my two sleepy little ones and three carry-on suitcases. Yes! I had a carry-on for each one of us, not even kidding.

My dad was eager to come meet us in Amman and take us home himself because he could not wait 8 more hours in addition to the 5 years since we had last saw him when he visited Chicago. Our six huge suitcases and three carry-ons were the only reason he did not meet us there! His car wouldn't fit that many suitcases along with three passengers. Knowing my dad, there was no way to stop him from meeting us in Amman if it had not been for that.

Diya, Lana, and I spent six hours in transit in Amman's airport. I was so exhausted trying to keep the kids entertained without losing any of them or our belongings.

When they called our plane, I felt a sense of relief and excitement. "Finally! We get to rest on the plane and shortly after I will be reunited with my family!," I thought to myself. Some of them I had not seen since I left Syria eight years prior. I did not realize how much I truly missed Syria until I exited the plane in Damascus.

We had been going down the stairs of the plane, on our way to the bus that would then take us to the gate, when Diya and Lana asked "Mama, are we in Sham (as we Damascenes call Damascus)?"

I responded while smiling ear to ear, "Yes, we are! Can't you smell the air?! It is Syria, it is Sham."

At that moment, I realized how much I had missed Damascus. I realized how much I loved everything there! Of course, I did! It is my homeland; it is the place my soul chose to arrive to mother earth at.

I literally loved everything - even the parts of the airport I had hated before! Everything put a smile on my face.

As we exited the gate to meet our family, I was brought back to the day I had left them 8 years earlier. Everyone was in that same place and the only difference was ME. I had left as a fresh college graduate, newlywed, to come back as a single mom with two little angels who had become my whole world.

Diya and Lana were overwhelmed by the size of our family in Syria. Any time they would meet a new person, my father would identify them as "family." In Syria, family was everywhere. This was very different than what they had experienced since birth. In Chicago, the only family they knew was me. No one else!!

When they got into my brother's car, they immediately fastened their seatbelts. My brother then turned back with a confused look on his face and asked, "What are you doing?" He burst into laughter. It was his first time meeting them, other than the occasional skype call. They innocently said, "putting our seatbelts." He then replied, "Do not worry about that, because more people are riding with us." That is Syria! We do not have the luxury of personal space. A car is usually overloaded with as many family members as can fit to get to the desired destination. This might sound miserable to some, but it is one of the simple joys of life in Syria.

When we visited my grandpa's farm in the Northwest Damascus suburbs - the place we spent our summers, spring breaks, and winter breaks at as children- I recognized how much I missed the color of that soil which is noticeably different than the color of soil in Chicago.

I also recognized that Chicago doesn't have the beautiful mountains that Syria has. It amazed me that I lived 8 years in Chicago and did not notice that *Chicago doesn't have mountains.*

I did not even feel how much I missed Syria until I went back. Did I not have feelings?! Perhaps I was drained from working fulltime, pursuing my master's degree, and raising my two kids as a single mom with no support system nearby.

Yes! That is a valid reason, I guess! My heart goes out to all of you single parents out there who refuse to give up your responsibilities of supporting and raising your children regardless of having the other parent's support or not.

THE SYRIA DAY OF RAGE

In 2008 I thought I knew what homeland meant. Well, when the revolution started in March of 2011, I realized that I did not know what homeland really meant.

At that time, I was working in corporate America as a staff accountant. I was planning to take my CPA exams to start my own Tax and Accounting firm so that I could spend more time with my kids before they grew up and had no time for me.

Early January of 2011 - I remember it vividly- my Facebook feed filled with celebratory posts for the Tunisians that had earned their freedom. I did not know what was happening then, because I was not the type to follow the news. Never understood it nor wanted to.

A few days later, my timeline turned into news about the revolution that had erupted in Egypt! I had so many Egyptian friends that I had met at work. And personally, like many other Middle Eastern and North Africans, Egypt meant a lot to me. At that time, I had never been to Egypt, but I had always dreamed of going there.

Egypt has a special place in my heart. My parents always told me about their honeymoon there, and I always enjoyed flipping through their photos by the pyramids, at the zoo, and other cool places there.

I followed the news coming from Egypt closely and interacted with it. Within less than thirty days, the great news broke:

the regime had been overthrown! It was such an exciting time for everyone. I remember that we went to celebrate with our Egyptian friends by the Egyptian Consulate in Chicago. The joy radiating from everyone was overwhelming as we carried a "Happy Valentine's Egypt" sign.

Following the event in Egypt, I came across a Facebook page for Syria! There was an English and Arabic page. I wanted to follow those pages, but I was worried. I did not want to do something that would put my family or myself in danger, since I did not yet understand what was happening. I decided to create a Facebook account with a fake name just to follow those pages and watch. Knowing the Syrian Regime, it was dangerous to speak out against anything we did not agree on. People can go to jail, get killed, tortured, or exiled for speaking their opinion. We grew up with that fear built in.

When the first peaceful protest started in Damascus, Dar'aa, and other cities around Syria, it only took a few days for the regime to start killing people. Very soon after, people started fleeing the country to escape the violence.

At that time, I was still working as a staff accountant in corporate America and studying to take my CPA exams.

I could not focus on studying anymore. I also started hating my job because I did not want to do anything that did not involve helping Syria nor did I want to miss any news while at work. I did not know what to do! Being a single mom, I could not just easily leave my job and focus on helping Syrians. I have to support my kids and myself.

As I observed the news, I connected with a few people around the US who had the courage to speak publicly about the event in Syria. We decided to join forces and organize a fundraising event to help the refugees. The place chosen for this event was Chicago, and since I am a local Chicagoan, I was responsible for most of the planning.

One of my tasks was to find a non-profit that can agree to raise funds for Syria and implement a program to help the refugees. We wanted to make sure we did everything legally and by the book to avoid any unnecessary trouble. I was referred to an organization via a close friend who agreed to help.

The event was very successful, and we were able to raise more than $150,000. After that event, the leader of that organization asked me to come on board to help with their work in the Middle East. The joy and gratitude I felt at that time cannot be expressed by words. I could not have asked for more!

God heard and answered my prayers within 3 months only. Now I can do what I wanted to do for a living.

THE RISING NON-PROFITS

Soon after the start of the revolution in March 2011, I have seen so many people starting their own nonprofit organizations. Back then it seemed like every Syrian wanted to start their own organization to help the people back in their hometown or provide specific aid such as supporting orphans, building schools, and so on.

Everyone who started a new organization got a lot of criticism. Many people wondered, *"Why wouldn't they just support the existing organizations?"*

On the other hand, the people who started their own organizations did not feel that supporting the existing organizations would fulfill the mission they envisioned.

Or maybe those organizations did not help the area they wanted to help. Perhaps they did not like the path other existing organizations were taking to help.

As I am writing this book in 2023, some organizations still exist and have grown a lot, while others have shutdown, or have not experienced much growth at all.

At that time, we Syrians thought we were the only community where each one of us wanted to have their own individual organization.

As I started working with more non-profits across the country from different backgrounds, I realized that regardless of their background, there were many individuals that wanted to start their own non-profit organization with their own unique mission in mind.

In fact, right now I think that starting your own nonprofit can be a great thing if you understand what it truly entails, and you are ready to pay the price that comes with it.

Most people start their nonprofit because of a temporary motivation, but they do not know what it is going to involve, what they will have to do, and how.

That is why I wanted to write this book —for you to see the full picture and decide if you want to start your own nonprofit organization or if you simply want to support another existing one.

There is no right or wrong answer. You are the only one who is qualified to make this decision.

My intention is to show you the full picture of what starting a nonprofit organization entails so you can make an informed decision and to guide you should you decide to start one.

MOTIVATIONS

You may have personally undergone a life-altering event or observed someone dear to you face a tremendous challenge. This encounter has served as a catalyst, igniting a deep sense of inspiration to lend a helping hand to others who may find themselves in similar circumstances.

Perhaps you were driven by a dissatisfaction with what you have observed in your surroundings, as well as the world at large, and you felt compelled to become the driving force of change. Your determination to create a meaningful impact in the lives of others, whether they are humans, animals, or plants, burns brightly within you. Fueled by this fiery passion, you embarked on a research journey, exploring the intricacies of establishing a charitable organization. Your eagerness to make a difference and effect positive transformation is apparent and inspiring.

Pause for a moment!

Before you proceed any further, it is crucial to take a moment and reflect upon a series of questions:

1. Are you truly determined to embark on the journey of establishing a charitable organization?

Take a moment to truly reflect on your intentions. Is this merely a fleeting motivation or an emotionally driven decision? Or is it something you genuinely aspire to pursue? It is crucial to make a responsible and informed decision, fully aware of what it entails and prepared to shoulder the responsibilities that lie ahead. There is no shortcut or easy way around it.

Recognize that starting a nonprofit is akin to launching a business, but with added challenges of working harder, acquiring greater knowledge, and making more substantial investments to achieve the desired impact while adhering to regulatory requirements.

Alternatively, you might consider exploring the option of joining an existing organization that shares your cause. By getting involved and providing support within your means, you can still contribute significantly to the cause without necessarily starting your own nonprofit.

Your answer is: 1. Yes. 2. No.

2. Are you prepared to assume the responsibility associated with starting a nonprofit?

Starting a nonprofit entail shouldering the responsibility for every action taken, whether you choose to run it on a full-time basis or serve as a board member at the very least. It becomes crucial to ensure proper structuring, well-crafted bylaws, and diligent enforcement of governance policies to safeguard not only yourself but also other board members and donors.

Your answer is: 1. Yes. 2. No.

3. Are you willing to strike a balance between protecting yourself and enabling the organization to flourish and make a positive impact? Alternatively, do you possess an unwavering commitment to protecting yourself to

the extent that it hampers the organization's growth and potential impact?

Be honest in your response and consider consulting with professionals to ensure you are fully prepared to embrace this responsibility.

Your answer is: 1. Yes. 2. No.

4. Are you willing to dedicate the necessary time and effort to start the organization and to run it as a business?

I have witnessed numerous individuals embark on starting a nonprofit organization with the misconception that everything will be readily available at no cost. They assume that volunteers will flock to offer their time, money, and services to help propel the organization's growth. However, the reality is that when you establish a non-profit, you are essentially establishing a business governed by specific tax regulations. The government grants tax benefits to individuals who support your cause, but in return, they expect heightened reporting, professionalism, and increased investment in the operation of your nonprofit.

If you find this hard to believe, I will explain the requirements for starting a nonprofit later in this book. For now, let me emphasize that starting a nonprofit goes beyond simply registering at the state level and obtaining an Employer Identification Number (EIN).

The journey does not end there when you choose to embark on the path of starting a nonprofit.

Your answer is: 1. Yes. 2. No.

5. Are you ready to take the risks involved in running a nonprofit organization?

It is important to be aware that while managing a nonprofit, you are entrusted with public funds, which are essentially contributions that could have been collected as taxes. Consequently, your organization operates under significant scrutiny, with much of its information accessible to the public.

Running a nonprofit carries substantial risk, as the consequences can be severe, potentially leading to legal ramifications, including the risk of facing imprisonment.

Your answer is: 1. Yes. 2. No.

6. Are you ready to become a lifelong student, eager to acquire knowledge that will help you with your new venture?

When embarking on a new endeavor, you are faced with a fundamental choice. The first option is to jump right into the experience, immersing yourself in hands-on learning. This approach involves investing your time and financial resources, adapting your strategies along the way, and being prepared to face the potential consequences of your decisions. While this path allows for experiential learning and the acquisition of valuable insights, it often demands a significant amount of time and effort before you can achieve your desired goals. It's important to acknowledge that success is not guaranteed, and you might never arrive to your desired destination.

Alternatively, you can proactively choose to educate yourself before and during your nonprofit journey. This involves seeking guidance from experienced mentors, engaging the services of coaches who can provide personalized support, and consulting with experts in the field. By tapping into the knowledge and expertise of others, you can navigate the path more efficiently, minimizing the likelihood of errors and setbacks. This approach allows you to benefit from the wisdom and lessons learned by those who have already walked a similar path.

Moreover, adopting a mindset of continuous learning is crucial. Recognizing that the world of nonprofits is constantly evolving, staying in the know of current trends, best practices, and innovations is essential for the sustained growth and impact of your organization. Embracing a commitment to ongoing education ensures that you remain open to new ideas, expand your knowledge base, and adapt your strategies accordingly. By doing so, you position your nonprofit for long-term success and the ability to make a lasting, positive impact on your chosen cause."

Your answer is: 1. Yes. 2. No.

7. Are you prepared to invest your time and create the necessary space for your organization?

Let's first address the space within your life before considering physical space. Can you dedicate one to two hours per day to your nonprofit? Or do you often find yourself lacking sufficient time for essential tasks? It's important to recognize that we are available for the things we prioritize.

Ultimately, it is your response to this question that matters, as you are on the brink of starting your nonprofit and investing daily hours is crucial for achieving the impact you desire.

If the programs you wish to establish require physical space, do you have access to such space, or do you possess the necessary resources and connections to make it available? While remote work is now prevalent, and even multimillion-dollar companies operate virtually from home, certain initiatives may require physical premises. Nevertheless, by employing creative thinking and problem-solving, you can often find alternative solutions. However, it is crucial to consider all aspects before proceeding with the registration of your organization.

Your answer is: 1. Yes. 2. No.

8. Are you willing to invest in your new project?

As I mentioned earlier, starting a nonprofit entail launching a business that demands both time and financial investments. Regardless of whether you choose to commit yourself full-time or part-time to the organization, it is crucial to recognize the importance of leveraging the time and expertise of others to ensure the success of your endeavors and the creation of the desired impact, all while maintaining compliance with relevant regulations.

While volunteers can play a valuable role in supporting your nonprofit's mission, relying solely on volunteer assistance is not a sustainable approach in the long run. Depending too heavily on volunteers may lead to challenges such as inconsistency, limited availability, and high turnover. This can result in operational difficulties, missed opportunities, and even the inability to fulfill your organization's objectives effectively.

To mitigate these risks and ensure the sustainability and growth of your nonprofit, it is essential to consider allocating resources for staffing, professional services, and other operational needs. This might involve hiring qualified individuals, seeking expert guidance, and making strategic financial investments to build a solid foundation for your organization.

By investing in your nonprofit, both financially and strategically, you demonstrate your commitment to its mission and increase the likelihood of achieving long-term success. It allows you to tap into the expertise and dedication of professionals who can help navigate challenges, optimize operations, and maximize the impact of your organization's work.

Your answer is: 1. Yes. 2. No.

9. Are you ready to sacrifice your privacy?

In the nonprofit world, maintaining privacy becomes a challenge as everything becomes a matter of public record. Starting a nonprofit means that almost every aspect of your organization will be publicly accessible. Your nonprofit's information, including its history since inception, can be found on the IRS website. This includes your nonprofit's annual tax returns (Form 990), which disclose details such as the names of officers and board members, the time dedicated to the organization, compensation of key team members, and much more.

It is crucial to understand that operating a nonprofit requires a high level of transparency. By entering this realm, you need to be prepared to surrender a certain degree of privacy. This commitment to openness not only upholds accountability but also helps foster trust with stakeholders and the public.

Your answer is: 1. Yes. 2. No.

Remember! Your nonprofit is a business and will only be successful if you run it as one.

If you answered "No" to any of the preceding questions, then you might want to STOP and find an organization that does what you wanted to do and support them instead.

You might say, "But Noura, I have my own way of doing things, and I do not like how other organizations operate!"

Okay! Then be a student, learn what you are about to get yourself into and start with crafting a business plan. Yes, a business plan! "Why?" you might ask. Simply because you are about to start a business with a nonprofit tax classification.

Let me warn you here, if you are not going to run your nonprofit like a business, you will FAIL! You will NOT be able to create the impact you are looking for. You will not be able to get the funds to support your programs, work full time in your organization, or to hire a good Executive Director and a team that is equipped to do the work and is in alignment with your mission.

REASONS WHY NON-PROFITS FAIL

In my opinion, the number one reason 50% of nonprofits fail is that the founder does not run it as a business.

According to the National Center on Charitable Statistics, the failure rate in the nonprofit sector is over 30% within the first 10 years!

From what I have observed, apart from the failure to run the nonprofit as a business, I would categorize them into three main sections:

1. Lack of Time
2. Lack of Money
3. Lack of Experience

Lack of Time

The founder of a nonprofit may have the experience but not the time to fully focus on their new organization. However, they still fail to leverage the time and experience of others to assist them. You must invest time in your new organization and allow it the necessary period to establish itself, implement programs, and demonstrate to the world the impact you can create.

By investing the necessary time, you provide your organization with the opportunity to grow, gain recognition, and make a tangible difference in the lives of those you aim to serve. It allows you to build strong foundations, foster partnerships, attract supporters, and establish credibility within the nonprofit sector.

Therefore, it is crucial to effectively leverage the time and expertise of others. Recognizing that your own time may be limited, seeking assistance, and involving others who are passionate about your cause can greatly enhance the effectiveness and efficiency of your organization, and potentially save it from failure.

Lack of Money

Starting a nonprofit, just like starting any other type of businesses, you must invest seed money to foster its growth.

Would you start a business without establishing a solid foundation? This foundation includes registration fees, market studies, consulting with professionals such as lawyers, accountants, and tax professionals. In addition, that seed money is essential to kick-start your first project.

Hopefully, your answer to that question was "No!"

Similarly, why would you expect to start a nonprofit with ZERO money thinking it would be successful?

Maybe you are thinking that people will offer pro bono services, or that you can rely solely on volunteers for everything.

Do you anticipate your business to grow by relying exclusively on pro bono work and volunteers? Do you expect experienced professionals to dedicate their time to work for free? Let me assure you, even if they wanted to, they would likely be occupied providing exceptional services to their paying clients, possibly even having a waitlist. Remember, donating services does not qualify for tax deductions; it is simply a gesture of goodwill. So, if you have come across posts on social media claiming that volunteering services can be tax-deductible, unfortunately, that is not true. Now you know!

You cannot foster the growth of a business with a scarcity mindset. To thrive, you must shift your mindset and infuse your organization with positive abundance energy. This involves being willing to compensate individuals for their work if you seek excellence and consistency. Let's consider this: are you expecting your board members to handle the workload? Well, that approach is rarely successful. Why? Simply because board members are volunteers who have their own obligations to support themselves and their families. They will never have the necessary time and capacity to devote to the organization.

Unfortunately, a scarcity mindset often dominates the nonprofit sector. Many individuals starting nonprofits believe they must offer their time and effort for free. They think everything must be obtained without cost, relying solely on volunteers. Consequently, they develop weak strategies, ineffective marketing, and poor financial management. As a result, they struggle to survive or expand their mission. Ultimately, they find themselves emotionally and financially depleted, experiencing disappointment and heartbreak. Not only are they unable to support their beneficiaries and fulfill their mission, but they also deplete their own emotional, financial, and temporal resources.

Lack of Experience

Like any other new endeavor, you wish to pursue, if you haven't done it before, it is highly likely that you will have to go through multiple trials and errors before achieving success. These trials and errors may span over years, require substantial financial investment, and often result in moments of heartbreak and more.

While it is true that a nonprofit is a business, knowing how to run a successful business does not necessarily guarantee success in running a nonprofit. Certain adjustments are crucial for your organization's success.

I have witnessed nonprofit leaders seeking guidance from other nonprofit leaders who have not achieved success themselves. This approach can be a recipe for disaster. It is essential to be discerning about the sources of your information and advice.

There are many misconceptions in the nonprofit world that you should be able to identify and avoid falling victim to. Staying informed and knowledgeable will help safeguard your organization against potential pitfalls.

COMMON NON-PROFIT MISCONCEPTIONS

Misconception #1: *Selling products with your nonprofit logo or awareness campaign is the way to get funded.*

I have seen so many organizations offering products be it t-shirts or other merchandise to generate income for their nonprofit. These organizations continue to struggle year after year, chasing a dream that will NEVER come true by relying on this approach.

While selling products can serve as a valuable tool for raising awareness and promoting your cause, it should not be relied upon as the primary means of generating funds. Consider the expenses incurred in purchasing the products, printing costs, as well as the time, effort, storage, and shipping involved. What is left for your organization to utilize? In most cases, it amounts to mere pennies or a few dollars.

Is it truly worth the investment of your time and money? Not only that, but you may also find yourself dealing with Unrelated Business Income Tax (UBIT), which adds an additional financial burden by requiring taxes to be paid on sales.

As I mentioned before, it is not worth it.

Misconception #2: *A majority of your nonprofit's funding will come from grants.*

I have witnessed many people seek out grant writers immediately after receiving their tax exemption letter, or start writing grants themselves, filled with excitement and eager to secure funding.

Unfortunately, most of them end up wasting time and money, only to face rejection after rejection. Funders typically require organizations to establish themselves and prove their capabilities before considering significant funding. This includes demonstrating the ability to raise funds, manage resources effectively, and create a measurable impact.

Would a bank grant you a mortgage without you providing two years of tax returns, a stable and consistent income, and a good credit report? I do not think so! Why should funders provide you with funding without a similar level of supporting evidence?

Would you lend money to someone without proof of how they manage their finances? That proof comes in the form of financial statements, evidence of impact, and the organization's tax return (990).

So how do you fund your organization?

Before you even think of applying for grants, you should start with growing your donor base. According to the Giving USA 2023 Report, approximately 64% of funding for nonprofits in the United States in 2022 came from individual donors. Individual donations would constitute as unrestricted funding unlike grants which would be classified as restricted funding.

Individual donations serve as your true foundation, providing a reliable source of support regardless of economic conditions. Nonprofits has been proven to be recission proof, and inflation proof due to the loyalty of donors. During challenging times, we tend to think of others who are suffering and find happiness and peace by helping them. Donors are the valuable treasure of your nonprofit.

I'm not suggesting that you should neglect grant funding. All I'm emphasizing is the importance of preparing yourself for grants before investing significant time and resources in pursuing them. Remember, grants make up only around 30% of your funding.

Misconception #3: *People do not have money to donate.*

The average person in the US donates $5,931, which equates to nearly $500 per month. With just 20 individuals contributing $500 to your organization each month, you could achieve $10,000 in monthly donations.

You may be skeptical, thinking that the people around you do not have the financial means to contribute. However, it is a fact that people at various income levels still donate to charity, whether they earn $13,000 per year or over $200,000 per year. Everyone possesses a willingness to give donations because, let's face it, there is a profound sense of personal fulfillment when you contribute to helping others. Who wouldn't want to experience that wonderful feeling?

Giving to charity is an act that each one of us, including children, engages in. I cannot express how many times my kids have approached me after being picked up from school or a community center, excitedly sharing that they have donated money to a cause. As a parent, regardless of my current financial situation, I always respond by praising their action because I want to instill in them the value of generosity. I'm certain that you share the same sentiment and approach as a parent.

I understand that not everyone can contribute $500 per month to charity. However, this means that you simply need to expand the number of people who support your cause. Every dollar makes a difference! It's important to provide an opportunity for those who are able to donate more to do so.

Income Range (AGI)	% of income given to charity
Under $15,000	13%
$15,000 - $29,999	8%
$30,000 - $49,999	7%
$50,000 - $ 99,999	5%
$100,000 - $199,999	3%
$200,000 - $249,999	3%

[1] Carlos, Alvin. "How Much Should You Donate to Charity in 2023?" *District Capital Management*, 17 Mar. 2023, districtcapitalmanagement.com/how-much-should-i-donate-to-charity/.

Misconception #4: *Nonprofits should be run by volunteers.*

Let me ask you this: would you run your business relying solely on volunteers? Would you be willing to go to work without receiving any compensation because the founder expects you to volunteer, or perhaps because you align with the business's mission?

I understand that you have a busy life, balancing family, work, and other commitments. How much time do you realistically have available for volunteering? I encourage you to contemplate these questions and answer them honestly.

I'm certain that you have very limited time available, if any. Considering this, do you believe that the time you have would be sufficient for volunteering in an organization that does not provide compensation? If your answer is yes, how long do you think you can sustain such a commitment? How professional can you realistically be in that capacity? Moreover, how successful do you think an organization can be if it primarily relies on individuals like yourself who volunteer their time? Additionally, how many people like you do you think would be able to volunteer their time, and for how long?

Please note that I am not suggesting that you should not have volunteers or that people should not volunteer. There is definitely a time and place to utilize volunteers. However, it is not feasible nor advisable to run an organization solely based on volunteers.

You need to have a system in place to effectively manage volunteers before you start utilizing them. This includes addressing the following aspects:

- Identifying how you will recruit volunteers.

- Implementing Standard Operating Procedures (SOPs) to ensure consistency within your organization, particularly when multiple individuals are performing similar tasks.

- Having clear job descriptions in place.
- Establishing a streamlined onboarding and offboarding process.
- Identifying a team member who will be responsible for overseeing volunteers.

Things to remember when working with volunteers:

- Do not allow volunteers to store organization-related documents on their personal computers. Instead, provide a shared & secure drive where they can save their work instantly. This ensures that the work is not lost due to a volunteer's absence or unavailability. It also ensures that sensitive organizational documents are stored securely.

- Volunteers are not there to run your organization; they are there to lend you a helping hand.

- Do not rely on volunteers for critical tasks or tasks that require professional expertise.

- Do not provide volunteers with a receipt for donating their time, as currently, at the time of writing this book, the IRS does not allow a tax deduction for volunteering time.

Misconception #5: *To keep overhead costs low, I should not hire staff.*

In simple terms, overhead costs refer to the operating expenses associated with running your organization. While these costs are necessary for the success of a nonprofit, not everything that is perceived as overhead truly falls into that category. Many expenses can actually be classified as program costs, despite some individuals considering them as overhead.

You should definitely consult with your accountant or CFO (Chief Financial Officer) regarding this matter. However, it is important to ask yourself a critical question: If I don't have this person on my team, can I still effectively run or implement this program? If the answer is no, then that expense should be considered a program expense rather than overhead.

For example, if the program you want to implement is delivering food to domestic violence survivors in a specific area, you need to assess the necessary components to determine if an expense is considered overhead. If you rely on a driver to deliver the food, you might initially think that their compensation falls under overhead. However, ask yourself this: Can you successfully implement the program without delivering the food? The answer is no, indicating that the driver's compensation should be classified as a program expense, not overhead.

If the driver is an employee or a contractor who also performs other tasks within the organization, it is important to evaluate their responsibilities and allocate expenses accordingly. By doing so, you can determine the percentage of expenses attributable to each program and identify any potential overhead.

Therefore, don't hesitate to hire staff and/or contractors as necessary, as they are crucial for the effective implementation of programs and the appropriate allocation of expenses.

Misconception #6: *We must deplete the organization's bank account each year.*

I have heard this sentiment from many nonprofit leaders: "We have to spend all of our cash before the end of the year!" However, if you exhaust your cash each year, where will your operational reserves come from? How will you pay your staff, contractors, and other expenses? How will you continue running your programs effectively? What about emergency relief efforts, if your organization is involved in that?

I'm not sure where this notion origi-
nated. It could be related to certain grant
awards, where funders may require the
money to be spent within a specific
timeframe. That may be true for grants depending on their requirements. However, it
is not true for other types of funding, especially individual donations.

It is crucial to understand the importance of building and maintaining operational reserves for the long-term sustainability of your organization. This allows you
to weather unforeseen challenges, support
ongoing operations, and fulfill your mission
effectively.

Misconception #7: *Board members should
be fully involved in making all the decisions.*

While board members are essential
for checks and balances, obtaining

501(c)(3) status, and securing funding, they should not be the cause of a nonprofit's failure. Unfortunately, I have witnessed many organizations decline due to the actions of their board members. Often, board members become overly involved in every decision, hindering the organization's growth and preventing it from reaching its full potential.

Board members should primarily focus on governing, monitoring, facilitating, and occasionally assisting with fundraising efforts. Attempting to involve themselves in every aspect of daily processes, decision-making, and spending can be detrimental to the organization's success. Board members have other responsibilities and busy lives that limit their ability to be directly involved in day-to-day operations. As a result, they may lack firsthand knowledge of the challenges faced by the team responsible for daily operations.

I want you to take a look at prominent organizations like the American Red Cross and observe their board members. You will find that many of them are executives in major companies such as Apple and Google. Do you believe these executives are involved in the day-to-day operations or decision-making of such large organizations? I highly doubt it.

Now, does it start to make sense why these large organizations thrive while many others struggle to grow and may even face the risk of dissolution shortly after their establishment?

Misconception #8: *Nonprofits organizations do not have to pay taxes.*

Just because a nonprofit organization is classified as tax-exempt, it does not mean it is exempt from filing taxes. The tax-exempt status is primarily intended to provide tax benefits to donors when they contribute to the nonprofit. While the organization may not have to pay income taxes on these donations, it is still required to file annual informational returns, typically represented by one of the 990 series forms. Failure to file the 990 for three consecutive years can result in the revocation of the organization's tax-exempt status. Additionally, not filing the 990 on time in any given year may lead to penalties.

Furthermore, if the nonprofit has employees, it is necessary to meet payroll tax obligations and ensure timely payment.

That is why having a tax professional who is familiar with nonprofit tax law is important.

It is crucial to address misconceptions and ensure that you are fully aware of what you are getting yourself into. This will enable you to make an informed decision that will contribute to your future success.

WHAT TO EXPECT WHEN RUNNING A NONPROFIT

Once you have made the decision to start your own nonprofit, here are the steps you need to take. After developing a business plan, which doesn't have to be complicated and can be kept simple, you can proceed with the registration process.

A. State registration (Incorporation)

This process involves formally registering your organization with the appropriate state authorities to legally recognize it as a nonprofit entity. It entails choosing the appropriate legal structure based on the options available in your state.

B. Federal Registration

You will need to obtain an Employer Identification Number (EIN), also known as your organization's Tax ID number. This number will be used for various purposes, such as opening a bank account, filing tax forms, and applying for tax-exempt status.

C. Apply for Exempt Status

To obtain a 501(c)(3) tax-exempt status, you must submit an application to the IRS. This allows your donors to receive tax benefits for their contributions and enables your organization to take advantage of various benefits, such as exemption from paying sales taxes on office supplies and access to free versions of operational and marketing tools essential for running your organization. You can choose to apply using Form 1023 or Form 1023-EZ.

If you choose to utilize Form 1023-EZ, there are certain limitations to consider. Your organization cannot exceed $50,000 in annual gross receipts, and your total assets must remain below $250,000. These criteria must be met to be eligible for the streamlined application process using Form 1023-EZ.

While the initial financial commitment for using Form 1023-EZ may be lower compared to Form 1023, I do not recommend opting for Form 1023-EZ due to its limitations. By choosing Form 1023, you can have the opportunity to scale your organization quickly and effectively. Why delay taking your organization seriously for three years? Your motivation and inspiration are present now, and waiting may dampen your enthusiasm. Therefore, I advise pursuing Form 1023 to fulfill your mission, make a significant impact, and ensure compliance with the IRS.

Application	1023 EZ	1023
Fees	$275	$600
Funding Limitation	≥$50,000	Unlimited
Asset Limitation	≥$250,000	Unlimited

Note: The application for exempt status can only be submitted electronically through pay.gov

COMPLIANCE

State Charity Registration

Let's return to the state where you incorporated your organization. Check the website of your state's attorney general to understand the steps required to be recognized as a tax-exempt charitable organization in your state. You can access the specific requirements for your state through this link https://www.irs.gov/charities-non-profits/state-links

Charitable Solicitation Registration

Before you start collecting funds, it is important to check with the states where you plan to raise funds to determine if you are required to register for a charitable solicitation. For more information, you can refer to the map provided by harboercompliance.com.

Charitable solicitation registration and disclosure statement required

Chariable solicitation registration required

Disclosure statement required

Not required (but other solicitation laws may apply)

www.harborcompliance.com

READY FOR THE IM-PACT

Now that you have all the necessary elements in place, it's time to start raising funds to implement your first program. But how do you go about doing that effectively? Think about the messages you receive asking for support from various individuals or organizations. Oftentimes, you may hesitate to contribute if the message lacks professionalism or doesn't come from a reliable and trustworthy source.

Therefore, it is crucial to present your organization as professional, reliable, and trustworthy. This starts with having a dedicated website and a seamless way to accept donations. Starting a website has become easier than ever, and it doesn't have to be overly complex. Even a simple landing page with a donation button can suffice initially until you have the resources to develop a more comprehensive website.

Additionally, it is important to have a professional email address that corresponds with your organization's name. Using an email address like @yourorganizationname.org instead of a generic @gmail.com or @yahoo.com creates a more professional image and instills trust in potential donors.

You want to ensure that your social media content looks professional. While you don't need to be present on every social media platform, it's important to be active on the platforms where your potential ideal donors are most likely to be found. By having these essential components in place, you can leverage them to effectively connect with potential donors and facilitate meaningful engagement. These elements will do much of the heavy lifting for you as you embark on your fundraising journey.

Once you have everything in place and you are ready to operate, you need to make sure you build your organization's capacity to ensure its sustainability, compliance, and preparedness for significant funding opportunities.

As a nonprofit you will need to have:

1. Board Members

Board members should be responsible for establishing the policies and the governance system, monitoring the overall organization, and evaluating the performance of the executive director. They should avoid micromanaging or making decisions unless they are major decisions that are not governed by any pre-approved policies.

2. Employees

Employees are essential to run your nonprofit effectively. The first paid employee should be the executive assistant who will help you implement your strategies and process the daily important tasks. They will help you grow your organization to a level where you can focus on managing your organization full time. The second paid employee should be the executive director who could be you or anyone you deem fit.

3. Consultants

By working with experienced professionals, you can receive a higher Return on Investment (ROI). Hiring consultants can be a great strategy to grow your organization and can help you save money that would otherwise be spent on payroll taxes, Paid Time Off (PTO), and benefits. Examples of consultants you may consider hiring include a coach, branding consultant, grant writer, accountant, CFO, and marketing consultant.

4. **Volunteers**

While volunteers can be very helpful for certain tasks, it is not advisable to rely solely on them. It is important to have someone who can manage and hold volunteers accountable. Additionally, you should be prepared for any potential volunteer absences. Critical tasks should not be assigned to volunteers, and it is important to ensure that they do not save any documents outside of the organization's shared drive. While this is also applicable to staff members, it is particularly critical for volunteers.

5. **Policies and Procedures**

   You need to have policies in place, including Standard Operation Procedures (SOP) and a training process for every task to ensure that your organization operates in a professional and consistent manner. Do NOT overlook the financial control policy, as this is one of the most important policies for your organization.

   In the beginning, you can start running your organization with your board members and yourself, and then gradually add a part-time assistant as soon as you are able. If you choose to operate virtually, it is important to obtain a virtual address rather than using your home address for professional purposes.

You want to start with the end in mind. Even when you are managing your organization alone, it is important to act as if you already have a team in order to build a strong organizational culture. By doing so, you will make the transition to working with a team much smoother when the time comes for you to seek assistance.

WHY IS CAPACITY BUILDING IM-PORTANT?

The IRS has a list of all organizations who have had their exempt status revoked in the past! After all the effort you put into registering your organization and applying for tax exempt status, it can be disheartening to find out that you may have to start over. This list is publicly available, and anyone can access it here:

https://www.irs.gov/charities-non-profits/charitable-organizations/revocations-of-501c3-determinations

Remember, when you start a non-profit, you are signing up to do something the government would otherwise have to address. That is why you are granted the privilege of tax exemption.

When taxpayers choose to donate to your organization and support your cause, they receive tax deductions.

As a result, you must adhere to numerous rules and regulations because you are handling public funds, and the IRS would be forgoing revenue of tax money.

This is a serious matter, and it's crucial to recognize the gravity of your obligations and treat them with the seriousness they deserve.

The good news is that you have the opportunity to reinstate your exempt status. However, the bad news is that the process can be costly, not to mention the fact that the revocation will remain on your record permanently.

In order to effectively manage your organization and meet the required standards, it is essential to build the capacity of your organization.

Do NOT lose your organization's exempt status!

Losing your exempt status can have severe consequences, including the loss of donations and other forms of funding. Donors are often motivated by the tax deduction they receive when donating to a charitable organization. If you are unable to offer that benefit, donors may choose to support another organization that can provide it.

Furthermore, losing your exempt status sends a message to donors that you are not taking your organization seriously. Why should donors entrust their hard-earned money to an organization that does not prioritize its own compliance and credibility? Just as you would hesitate to invest in a business run by someone who does not take it seriously, donors may question their trust in your organization.

Additionally, a revocation of your exempt status can negatively impact your ability to secure grant funding. Funding opportunities often require organizations to have a valid and active exempt status. Losing this status may exclude you from valuable grants, limiting your organization's financial resources.

To avoid these detrimental outcomes, it is crucial to take the necessary steps to maintain your exempt status and uphold the standards expected of nonprofit organizations.

It is up to you not to lose your exempt status!

In order to maintain your nonprofit's tax-exempt status, make sure the following documents are easily accessible:

1. Permeant Records
    a. Organizing Documents
    b. Form 1023
    c. Determination letter (This is the 501(C)(3) that you received as the approval for exempt status)
2. Annual Filings & Record used to prepare returns:
    a. Description of your organization's programs
    b. Meeting minutes of governing board and any standing committees

3. Documenting Financial Records (Bookkeeping)
    a. Income: save these records for 3 years after the return is due or filed whichever is later
    b. Expenses: save these records for 3 years after the return is due or filed whichever is later
    c. Employment Tax Records: save these records for at least 4 years
    d. Asset Records: keep document for as long as you own the asset plus 3 years after you dispose of the item

Note: If your organization has multiple programs, you should track your income and expenses for each program separately.

Are you ready to treat bookkeeping & record keeping as a requirement in order to stay in compliance—rather than treating it as luxury as many think it is?

The following activities can jeopardize your exempt status:

- Not filing Form-990 for 3 consecutive years
- Lobbying
- Political campaign intervention
- Activities generating excessive unrelated business income (UBIT)
- Private benefit
- Inurement: Allowing income or asset to accrue for the benefit of insiders

Everything I have mentioned so far is focused on preparing your organization for operation and ensuring compliance. You have not yet started collecting donations or pursuing any funding opportunities. We also have not addressed program implementation or management.

However, the good news is that technology is available to assist you if you are ready to utilize it and harness its potential to support your organization.

Must have tools:

1. **Accounting and Bookkeeping Software**

   This tool, if utilized correctly, will help you stay in compliance. Furthermore, it will ensure you are prepared for tax filing, funding acquisition, and audits. On top of that, it will enable you to make informed financial decisions. Be ready to file your taxes, acquire funding, and financial audits.

2. Donor Management System

I find it concerning that many people overlook this aspect and fail to prioritize it. Your donors are the livelihood of your organization, ensuring a steady cash flow that enables you to make the impact you envisioned when you started. It is crucial to have comprehensive data on each current and potential donor, including the timing, method, and amount of their contributions. This data will aid in planning future fundraisers. In fact, your objective should be to secure enough recurring donations to operate your organization as a sustainable and scalable entity. Relying solely on Excel won't suffice for this task.

CONCLUSION

In conclusion, if you are prepared to shoulder the responsibility, invest your time, money, and effort, take calculated risks, embrace a learning mindset, have the necessary physical and mental space, value transparency over privacy, treat your organization as a business, adopt an abundance mindset, engage with your ideal donors and ask for financial support, stay compliant to avoid revocation, and take on multiple roles or hire someone to fill those roles, then you are ready to embark on the journey of starting and running a nonprofit organization.

If you comprehend all of the considerations and remain committed to making a meaningful impact by implementing your distinct vision, assuming all associated responsibilities, then proceed with starting your own nonprofit. It is an opportunity for you to share your unique vision, knowledge, and expertise in creating a positive impact. However, if you are not prepared for such a venture, it is advisable to find an existing organization to support and engage with as a volunteer, contributing your time when available. Avoid starting an organization that may not thrive or potentially put you in challenging circumstances, all in the pursuit of an impact that you may not be able to sustain.

If you are prepared to assume the responsibility but feel apprehensive about starting alone and desire support throughout your journey, consider joining a coaching program that offers guidance, assistance, and a well-defined roadmap to help you navigate the process.

I work with nonprofit leaders to help them build a successful organization through my 7-figure nonprofit mastermind. You can apply to join my program by visiting this link:

https://www.nourasbooks.com/Nouras7FNPM

Having a coach is essential as they can provide you with shortcuts to reach your goals, hold you accountable, and offer support during challenging times on your journey.

Most, if not all, successful individuals you hear about have a coach or even multiple coaches. I came to recognize the significance of having a coach when I embarked on my own firm in 2021. Even before generating any income from my business, I made the proactive choice to engage a coach, and it proved to be the most remarkable decision I've ever made. Upon implementing the strategies recommended by my coach, I started generating income right away.

When embarking on your own venture, whether it be a company or a nonprofit organization, it is crucial to prioritize your mindset. You must challenge and overcome any limited beliefs and prevent misconceptions from dictating your actions and operations. If the prevailing notions about nonprofits were true, we would witness tens of thousands of thriving organizations surpassing the $5,000,000 funding mark, and the world would be a significantly better place than it currently is. However, as we know, this is not the case. Therefore, if you aspire to build a successful organization, it is imperative to do what is right and refrain from blindly following the opinions of the masses.

I want to emphasize a crucial point: joining a coaching program does not guarantee automatic success or funding. It requires your unwavering commitment to putting in the necessary work and diligently implementing the strategies you learn along the way. Patience and consistency are key factors in achieving tangible results.

I personally believe in the value of having a coach to support me in improving and scaling my business and personal life, and I encourage you to consider the same. You don't necessarily have to join my coaching program; instead, explore the available options that align with your specific needs and goals. The key is to find a coaching program that works best for you, enabling you to save time, money, and effort while making progress towards your desired impact.

Remember, be honest with yourself and evaluate whether starting a nonprofit is truly what you want to do or if you would prefer to support an existing organization.

If you have decided to start your own organization, I invite you to watch my free masterclass on how to get $10,000 for your nonprofit in 30 days. This masterclass will provide you with a framework to understand your responsibilities as a nonprofit leader. It is completely free, and you can watch it as many times as you want.

A GIFT

https://www.nourasbooks.com/freenon-profitmasterclass

ABOUT THE AUTHOR

Author Noura Almasri, M.Sc., EA

Noura Almasri is an Enrolled Agent with
the Internal Revenue Services, and the
founder and CEO of Noura's Books. She is
also an International Bestselling Author,
known for her expertise in helping

nonprofits increase funding through efficient process and regulatory compliance.

Noura holds a master's degree in business information technology from DePaul University. She has over 20 years of experience in accounting, gained from various corporations and her work in managing and growing nonprofit organizations. Throughout her career, she has served in diverse role creating and implementing managerial and financial strategies that have driven significant growth in the companies and organizations she has assisted.

In addition to her nonprofit work, Noura is dedicated to helping business owners achieve their financial goals by increasing cash flow.

Driven by her passion for making a difference, Noura founded Noura's Books, a virtual tax and accounting firm, with the aim of helping more individuals achieve their dreams while leaving a positive impact on their communities.